W9-BXY-822

Beetles

by Cheryl Coughlan

goldsmith beetle

Consulting Editor: Gail Saunders-Smith, Ph.D.

Consultant: Gary A. Dunn, Director of Education,
Young Entomologists' Society

Pebble Books

an imprint of Capstone Press
Mankato, Minnesota

Pebble Books are published by Capstone Press
818 North Willow Street, Mankato, Minnesota 56001
http://www.capstone-press.com

Library of Congress Cataloging-in-Publication Data
Coughlan, Cheryl.
    Beetles/by Cheryl Coughlan.
    p. cm.—(Insects)
    Includes bibliographical references (p. 23) and index.
    Summary: Simple text and photographs present the features and behavior
of beetles.
    ISBN 0-7368-0235-5
    1. Beetles—Juvenile literature. [1. Beetles.] I. Title. II. Series: Insects
(Mankato, Minn.)
QL576.2.C68 1999
595.76—dc21
                                                              98-52996
                                                                   CIP
                                                                    AC

Note to Parents and Teachers

The Insects series supports national science standards for units on the diversity and unity of life. The series shows that animals have features that help them live in different environments. This book describes and illustrates the parts of beetles. The photographs support early readers in understanding the text. The repetition of words and phrases helps early readers learn new words. This book also introduces early readers to subject-specific vocabulary words, which are defined in the Words to Know section. Early readers may need assistance to read some words and to use the Table of Contents, Words to Know, Read More, Internet Sites, and Index/Word List sections of the book.

Table of Contents

Beetles 5

Legs and Wings 11

Jaws and Eating 17

Note to Parents and Teachers . . . 2

Words to Know 22

Read More 23

Internet Sites 23

Index/Word List 24

4

Beetles can be
many colors.

six-spotted tiger beetle

6

Some beetles are small.

mealworm beetle

Some beetles are big.

female rhinoceros beetle

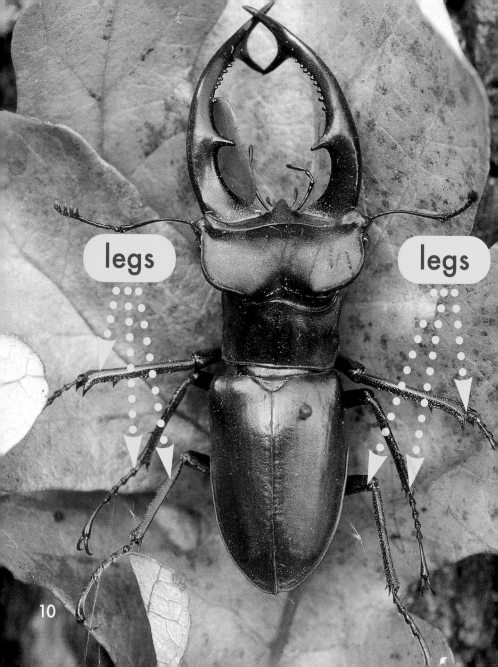

legs

legs

Beetles have six legs.

giant stag beetle

hard
wings

Beetles have
two hard wings.

golden net-wing beetle

soft wings

Beetles have
two soft wings.

longhorn beetle

jaws

Beetles have strong jaws.

reddish-brown stag beetle

Some beetles eat plants.

glorious June beetle

Some beetles eat insects.

fiery searcher beetle eating
gypsy moth caterpillar

Words to Know

insect—a small animal with a hard outer shell, three body parts, six legs, and two antennas; insects may have two or four wings.

jaw—a mouthpart used to grab things, bite, and chew; beetles' jaws move from side to side when they chew.

wing—a movable part of an insect that helps it fly; a beetle has hard front wings that cover soft back wings; the hard wings are called elytra and are not used for flying.

Read More

Gerholdt, James E. *Beetles.* Incredible Insects. Edina, Minn.: Abdo and Daughters, 1996.

Julivert, Maria Ángels. *The Fascinating ⸍⸍rld of Beetles.* Hauppauge, N.Y.: Barron's, 1995.

Stefoff, Rebecca. *Beetle.* Living Things. New York: Benchmark Books/Marshall Cavendish, 1997.

Internet Sites

Beetles
http://www.ent.iastate.edu/imagegal/coleoptera

Beetles
http://www.source.at/beetles

Meet the Beetles!
http://www.clpgh.org/cmnh/discovery/beetles

Tiger Beetle World
http://members.aol.com/YESedu/home.html

Index/Word List

beetles, 5, 7, 9, 11, 13, 15, 17, 19, 21
big, 9
colors, 5
eat, 19, 21
hard, 13
insects, 21
jaws, 17
legs, 11

many, 5
plants, 19
six, 11
small, 7
soft, 15
some, 7, 9, 19, 21
strong, 17
two, 13, 15
wings, 13, 15

Word Count: 39
Early-Intervention Level: 6

Editorial Credits
Martha E. Hillman, editor; Timothy Halldin, cover designer; Kimberly Danger, photo researcher

Photo Credits
Bill Johnson, 16
Connie Toops, 6
David Liebman, cover, 4, 10, 18
James P. Rowan, 1
Rob and Ann Simpson, 8, 20
Rob Curtis, 12, 14